The Dean's Message

I t is good to welcome all visitors to St.Paul's and I hope that this Guide will provide a happy reminder of your visit.

A Cathedral has stood on this site since the early years of the seventh century. Christopher Wren's masterpiece has been described as the most powerful architectural statement ever made in the City of London. But the ministry of St Paul's, while it is deeply routed in the life of the City and of the Diocese of London, extends throughout the world. It is a living, working symbol of Christian faith and witness.

Our English cathedrals stand at the forefront of the Church's mission. They work on the boundary of church and community life. They are in touch day by day with the large numbers of people who often have only an occasional relationship with the Church.

They are one aspect - and a tremendously important aspect - of the public face of the Church of England. Their work is primarily evangelism.

But the primary purpose of St Paul's is the worship of God, and the daily offering of prayer lies at the heart of all that we do. Find time during your visit to stop and be still. Allow the majesty of the building to speak of the majesty of God. It is always good to welcome those who come from all parts of the world. Thank you for your prayers and your generous support which enable us to take forward the mission of this Cathedral church.

John Moses, Dean of St. Paul's

Tour of the Cathedral

Your first view of St Paul's should be a memorable one, for the Cathedral represents inspiration, beauty and craftsmanship on a grand scale. Your entry by the West End (33/34) gives you the opportunity to look down the Nave (2) towards the Cathedral's crowning achievements: the Dome and the High Altar (4).

The architectural style of St Paul's is English Baroque, which combines classic lines with a strong sense of dynamic movement. This style was widely used in Europe during the 17th and early 18th centuries, but was a daring and controversial choice for an English cathedral. Several plans were offered by the architect, Sir Christopher Wren, before a design was eventually accepted by the King and even this Wren varied greatly as the building proceeded.

The central Great West Door behind you are opened for special occasions. Above them is the gallery from which triumphal 'Royal trumpet' fanfares ring out, for example during services for events of special or national importance.

Your suggested tour of the Cathedral begins in the South Aisle (5) of the Nave (to your right).

Above:
The altar in the Chapel of the Order of St Michael and St George (6).

Below:
Heraldic plaques commemorating Knights Grand Cross of the Order of St Michael and St George (6).

THE SOUTH AISLE

The Chapel in the South Aisle was dedicated in 1906 to the Order of St Michael and St George (6) – those who have been honoured for distinguished service to the Commonwealth or overseas. Banners of the Knights Grand Cross of the Order hang above the stalls, which also feature heraldic plaques. When a Knight dies, his banner is taken down and his plaque is fastened on the book rests as a memorial. The Throne opposite the altar incorporates carved 17th century cherubs. Behind the altar, the reredos features a statue of St George. In a niche below it is a sculpture of St Michael trampling on the seven deadly sins.

The monuments along the South Aisle mainly commemorate naval and military heroes. One notable exception is the monument to Thomas Fanshaw Middleton (1769-1822), the first Anglican Bishop of India. He is shown blessing two Indian children kneeling before him.

*The Nave, (2)
looking towards
the Dome and
High Altar (3/4).*

The Light of the World *(7)* by William Holman Hunt (1827-1910) is the most celebrated and famous painting in the Cathedral. It is the third version of the subject, painted some 50 years after the first which hangs in Keble College, Oxford. The painting was given to the Cathedral by Charles Booth in 1908 after it had been on a world tour – 'a sermon in a frame'. It shows Christ knocking at a humble door which, significantly, can only be opened from within. The artist is buried in the Cathedral Crypt.

THE SOUTH TRANSEPT

The Transepts, the shorter wings of a cathedral or church form the shape of the cross. The South Transept *(8)* contains tributes to national figures, including JMW Turner the painter (1775-1851) and the explorer Captain Robert Falcon Scott (1868-1912) and his companions who died on the return journey from the South Pole.

As befits a maritime nation, the South Transept holds a place of honour for Flaxman's

The Cathedral's most famous painting, The Light of the World by William Holman Hunt (7).

elaborate memorial to Admiral Horatio Viscount Nelson (1758-1805). It shows the naval hero leaning on an anchor, a draped cloak disguising his missing right arm.

The South Transept's chief glory is the doorcase, originally part of the Choir Screen and organ gallery. The carved garlands, cherubs and embellishments of the fluted columns are by the Anglo-Dutch master carver, Grinling Gibbons (1648-1721), an exceptionally talented sculptor whose craftsmanship was recognised by Wren and used widely throughout the building.

The small but striking bronze figure of Christ being released from the cross is a memorial to the 4,300 colonial troops of Australia, Canada, New Zealand, Ceylon and South Africa who died fighting for Britain in the 1899-1902 South African War. The sculptor was Princess Louise, daughter of Queen Victoria. Banners hanging in the South Transept are those of the Dominions of Australia, New Zealand and Canada together with that of the United Kingdom.

To one corner of the South Transept stands the first statue to be erected in St Paul's – to the philanthropist and campaigner for prison reform, John Howard (1726-90). He is represented in Roman costume holding a scroll which reads: Plan for the Improvement of Prisons and Hospitals.

Flaxman's memorial to Admiral Horatio Viscount Nelson (8).

THE MOSAICS

The mosaics on the spandrels between the arches of the Dome (3) were designed by G.F. Watts. Alfred Stevens and W.E.F. Britten and executed by the firm of Salviati in Venice on the island of Murano. They represent the four evangelists and four of the Old Testament prophets. Made of little square blocks (tesserae), the surface of these mosaics is flat and catches the eye by virtue of design, colour and gilding.

In 1891, William Blake Richmond was appointed to carry out the mosaic decoration of the Chancel or Quire (9). Richmond studied early mosaic methods which used irregularly-

Detail of the mosaic of angels around the saucer domes (9).

set reflecting glass tesserae to give brilliant and sparkling images. Thick slabs of opaque glass of various colours were produced by Messrs Powell of Whitefriars from which the tesserae for the mosaics were cut. The stone work of the Cathedral was cut away to a depth of just over two cms. and the tesserae were fixed into place.

The theme of the mosaics in the saucerdomes is that of the creation - birds of the air, fishes of the sea, beasts and cattle, all green things upon the earth, echoing that of the canticle "Benedicte" whose text is quoted in Latin in the Quire vault. Christ the King, with the Father in the Creation, is the central figure of the apse. A friese runs round the Quire, depicting Adam and Eve in Paradise and at peace with the animal kingdom, tigers, lions, peacocks and young panthers. Below, in the spandrels of the Quire is, on the south side, the story of the Fall, Adam and Eve being expelled from Paradise on the north side, the story of the redemption with the Angel Gabriel coming to Mary and the

angelic choirs celebrating the birth of Christ. On either side of the clerestory windows are kings and prophets, sybils and holy men, all looking for the coming of Christ, and illustrating the theme of the musical chants or antiphons sung by the choir in Advent at Evensong in the eight days running up to Christmas.

Top right:
Birds of the air mosaic (10).

Right:
The crowning mosaic above the High Altar of Christ the King (4).

The three saucer domes of the Choir ceiling celebrate God's creatures (9).

THE CHANCEL OR QUIRE

The Chancel or Quire *(9)* forms the top of the Cathedral's cross shape and is the most richly decorated part of the Cathedral interior. This part of the Cathedral was where Wren's workmen started building and was opened for worship on 2 December 1697. The first service was, appropriately, a thanksgiving for peace following the Treaty of Ryswick which marked the end of conflict between France and England. Henry Compton, Bishop of London, preached at the service from the text: "I was glad when they said unto me, let us go into the House of the Lord." In his term of office, Bishop Compton saw St Paul's rise from rubble to magnificent Cathedral over 35 years.

The Choir Stalls *(10)* are where the Choir and clergy sit during services. Its richly carved oak and limewood stalls are by Grinling Gibbons. Notable craftsmanship can be seen on the Bishop's Throne

Left:
The Chancel, the most richly decorated part of the Cathedral (9).

Below:
The carved oak and limewood choir stalls (10).

(11). Situated near to the High Altar on the south side, it is decorated with foliage and flowers, winged cherubs' heads and garlands. Within it is a high-backed chair which displays the arms of Bishop Compton.

The Prebendaries (referred to later in "Behind the Scenes") occupy the back row of the choir stalls. Prebendaries are required to recite part of the Psalter daily, and the Latin words on each stall remind them which part of the Psalter is their responsibility! Also on the north side can be seen the Lord Mayor of London's stall, which includes a rest for his sword. This stall is adorned with a delicately carved ornament of flowers and foliage, above which are the carved emblems of his office, a sword of justice and the mace to symbolise his authority.

The Cathedral's original organ *(12)* – Wren called it a 'box of whistles' – was built by 'Father' Schmidt and installed in 1695. It stood originally on a screen which divided the Quire from the nave. In the 1860s, the screen was removed, the organ was divided and enlarged and has since been improved and extended to

Above:
Detail of carving by Grinling Gibbons (10).

Main picture
The carved organ case, Wren's "box of whistles", and the brass eagle lectern dating from 1719 (12).

become the third largest organ in the country. The organ case carvings, which include large-scale figures (again by Grinling Gibbons) survived the modifications over the years, so that the quality of the sound and the beauty of the organ's decoration are two of the glories of the Cathedral. Handel and Mendelssohn both enjoyed playing it. Great skill and craftsmanship are needed by the organist who has to master the console of five keyboards, each with 61 notes and a pedalboard of 32 notes. There are 138 organ stops which operate a total of 7,189 pipes. The powerful trumpets, situated on the West

Gallery, are also played from the organ console.

To one side at the front of the Choir is the brass eagle lectern, made in 1719 by Jacob Sutton. The eagle is the symbol of the fourth Evangelist (St John) and became a convenient pattern for a reading stand on which to rest the Bible. (The other evangelists are represented by an ox (St Luke) a lion (St Mark) and the face of a man (St Matthew)).

To the other side of the Choir stands the carved oak and limewood pulpit (13), installed in 1964 to celebrate the 250th anniversary of the completion of the Cathedral. Sir Christopher Wren's original design for a pulpit had wheels so it could be moved around the building. The present one was designed by Lord Mottistone, Surveyor to the Fabric of St Paul's, 1957-63.

THE AMBULATORY

The walkway around the Chancel is called the Ambulatory. It consists of the North (14) and South Choir Aisles (15) and the Apse (16).

At the entrance to the Ambulatory (North Choir Aisle) stands a statue, around 4.5 metres high, commemorating Samuel Johnson, the famous 18th century literary figure best known for the dictionary he compiled and published in 1755. Although Johnson was buried in Westminster Abbey, John Bacon's memorial to him was unveiled in St Paul's two years later in 1796.

Nearby, at a spot chosen by the sculptor himself, is Henry Moore's modern masterpiece, Mother and Child (1984) carved from Travertine marble. It has been described as having "an elemental and yet eminently approachable quality, expressive of motherhood and compassion".

Exquisite wrought-iron gates (17) separate the aisles from the High Altar. They were made by Jean Tijou, a French master

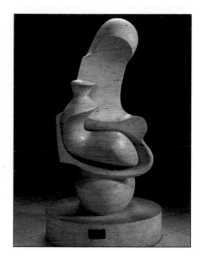

ironworker and one of the fine craftsmen Wren employed. Tijou was responsible for most of the ornamental ironwork in the Cathedral. These gates, together with those in the opposite aisle, are considered to be Tijou's best work in England.

The Chapel of Modern Martyrs (18) commemorates all known Anglican Martyrs who have died for their faith since 1850. Their names are recorded in a book which is displayed in a glass-topped marble casket. The crucifix over the alter is from the Victorian reredos of St Paul's, which was damaged by a bomb in 1940.

Above:
Henry Moore's modern masterpiece, Mother and Child, in the Ambulatory (14).

Below:
Tijou's wrought iron gates (17).

Right:
The High Altar topped by a massive carved oak canopy, dating from 1958 (4).

Far right:
The High Altar's cross stands nearly 3 metres high (4).

Bottom right:
The High Altar's crowning piece, the risen Christ, his right hand extended in blessing (4).

THE HIGH ALTAR

The present High Altar *(4)*, topped by a massive carved oak baldacchino or canopy, dates from 1958. The design echoes the pencil sketch of a baldacchino Wren envisaged as the focal point of his grand building. The 20th century version, considered an outstanding piece of craftsmanship, is a memorial from the British people to members of the Commonwealth forces who died during the two World Wars. The altar is made of a slab of Italian marble, weighing nearly four tonnes. It replaces the bomb-damaged and highly controversial 19th century High Altar, which in turn replaced the original. The massive cross stands nearly 3 metres high and the candlesticks, made of gilded and lacquered bronze coins, stand 1.6 metres high. The cross has an enamelled base of silver with amethyst and polished rock crystal at its centre. These ornaments were a gift from the Goldsmiths' Company. The crowning piece, above a gilded cupola, is a figure of the risen Christ, his right hand extended in blessing.

THE AMERICAN MEMORIAL CHAPEL

The small chapel in the Apse (or recess) behind the High Altar is now the American Memorial Chapel *(19)*. Two architects, Godfrey Allen and Stephen Dykes Bower, designed the restoration of the whole of this war-damaged east end of the Cathedral, including this Chapel. It was created as a British tribute to the 28,000 Americans based in Britain who lost their lives in the Second World War. The entire cost was met by donations from thousands of British men, women and children. The Roll of Honour, 500 pages of illuminated manuscript bound in red leather, was presented to St Paul's by General Eisenhower in 1951. The Chapel was dedicated in 1958 in the presence of Her Majesty the Queen and Richard Nixon, Vice-President of the United States.

The panelled limewood carvings of the birds, plants and flowers of America even include a modern space rocket hidden in the foliage in the panel on the far right. The three stained glass windows in this Chapel by Brian Thomas date from 1960 and depict the service, sacrifice and resurrection of the faithful soldier. Their borders carry the emblems of the States of America.

Right:
The American Memorial Chapel, dedicated in 1958 (19).

Below:
The Roll of Honour in the American Memorial Chapel (19).

SOUTH CHOIR AISLE

The Lady Chapel *(20)* in South Choir Aisle *(15)* was created as recently as 1959. The marble statue of the Virgin and Child behind the altar was once a part of the High Altar reredos in the 19th century. The oak surround originally belonged to Wren's great organ screen and the oak altar table was his original High Altar. The wooden crucifix and candlesticks are 18th century Bavarian, a gift from President Theodor Heuss of West Germany during his state visit to Britain in 1958.

The South Choir Aisle contains a bronze effigy of the distinguished historian and former Bishop of London, Mandell Creighton who died in 1901. The marble effigy of the most famous Dean of St Paul's *(21)*, John Donne (1573-1631), is by Nicholas Stone. Donne posed for this statue during his last illness wrapped in a sheet to represent the shroud. The effigy was the only figure from the Old St Paul's Cathedral to survive, intact, the

Great Fire of 1666. As the old Cathedral burned, the statue fell into the Crypt. Scorch marks can still be seen round the base. Donne wrote the much quoted words: "No man is an Island entire of itself: every man is a piece of the Continent, a part of the main... Any man's death diminishes me, because I am involved in Mankind: And therefore never send to know for whom the bell tolls; it tolls for thee."

The South Choir Aisle contains fragments from the Holy Land which are now fixed to the wall. They consist of a carved stone from Solomon's Temple, a carved piece of marble from Herod's Temple and a section of the Roman Pavement from Jerusalem. Nearby is the Processional Cross made for St. Augustine's Church, still carried by the senior chorister at all choir services.

Below:
The Lady Chapel in South Choir Aisle (20).

Bottom left:
Marble effigy to John Donne, which survived, intact, the Great Fire of 1666 (21).

THE DOME AND WHISPERING GALLERY

The central pavement area under the Dome (3) is decorated in a compass design in coloured marble and carries the Latin epitaph for Wren: "Beneath lies buried the founder of this church and city Christopher Wren, who lived more than ninety years not for himself but for the public good. Reader, if you seek his monument, look around you." The brass grille at the core is one of several set in the Cathedral's marble paving. It was a 19th century attempt to heat St Paul's. Stoves were lit in the Crypt below and hot air

Above:
Central pavement area under the Dome, with Wren's Latin epitaph (3).

Main picture:
The Dome, among the largest in the world (3).

Inset:
Detail of the Dome's fresco paintings by Sir James Thornhill (3).

from them rose through the metal gratings.

The Dome is among the largest in the world, comparable with St Peter's in Rome. The main structure is of Portland stone from Dorset. The Dome's weight (plus superstructure) is some 65,000 tonnes. Eight piers support it and eight arches spread the load of the Dome on to the piers. At the top of each arch is a keystone, carved by Caius Gabriel Cibber. Above them is the Whispering Gallery, so called because a whisper against the blank circular wall can be heard on the opposite

side, some 42 metres away. The Whispering Gallery is the best place to view the fresco paintings inside the Dome, painted by James Thornhill between 1716-19. The decorative metal railing is by Jean Tijou. Statues in niches above the Whispering Gallery represent the Early Fathers of the Christian Church. Above are the Stone and the Golden Galleries which give superb panoramic views of London.

There are 530 steps up to the Golden Gallery, while the height of the cross above it is 111 metres from the ground.

The Dome actually consists of three structures: the outer lead-

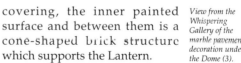

covering, the inner painted surface and between them is a cone-shaped brick structure which supports the Lantern.

When the Dome was being built, Wren was hauled up in a basket two or three times a week to see how work was progressing. By the time it was completed in 1708 he was 76 years old. He watched as his son fixed the last stone in position on the Lantern at the top of the cupola.

View from the Whispering Gallery of the marble pavement decoration under the Dome (3).

*The Italian
marble font,
dating from 1727
(24).*

NORTH TRANSEPT

Regular services are held in the North Transept, in which the colours of the Middlesex Regiment are displayed. Here the Blessed Sacrament is reserved in the aumbry, whose door was carved by our Master Carver, Anthony Webb in 1979. The carving on the door represents the pelican, who by tradition gives its own life for the sake of its children, a figure of Christ giving his life for the sake of humankind. Among the Middlesex Regiment colours on display is a staff with no banner. It represents the loss of one of the Regiment's colours at the fall of Hong Kong to the Japanese in 1941. Behind the altar is a 16th century Italian painting of The Holy Family (with St Luke and the painting's donor).

The font (24), by Francis Bird, dates from 1727 and is made from yellowish blue-veined Italian marble. Nearby is the celebrated memorial, by Sebastian Gahagan,

to General Thomas Picton (1758-1815), killed at the Battle of Waterloo. One of the simplest and most moving figures in the Cathedral is the terracotta Virgin and Child sculpture by Josephine de Vasconcellos (1957).

On a corner of the North Transept and North Aisle is a white marble figure, by John Flaxman, of Sir Joshua Reynolds (1723-1792), one of England's finest portrait painters who became first president of the Royal Academy.

Above:
John Flaxman's white marble figure of Sir Joshua Reynolds (23).

Left:
Terracotta Virgin and Child by Josephina de Vasconcellos, 1957 (23).

THE NORTH AISLE

On the wall of the North Aisle *(26)* are four alabaster plaques recording the Deans of St Paul's since 1066.

A glass case contains the roll of honour of the 33,000 members of the Merchant Navy and the fishing fleets who died while serving in the Second World War.

A notable work in the North Aisle is Baron Marochetti's monument to two successive Lords Melbourne: William (d 1848) who was Queen Victoria's first Prime Minister and his diplomat brother Frederick (d 1853). It depicts white marble sleeping angels at either side of the black marble and bronze doors of death.

Framed by a Nave arch is the towering monument *(27)* to the Duke of Wellington (1769-1852) who defeated Napoleon. The artist, Alfred Stevens, worked on this piece for 20 years and it was still incomplete on his death in 1875. The figure of the Duke on his horse Copenhagen was sculpted by John Tweed

The Duke of Wellington's memorial in the North Aisle (27).

Main picture:
The Chapel of St Dunstan featuring a mosaic composed after the manner of Raphael (28).

Inset:
Bronze effigy of Major General Charles Gordon (26).

and added in 1912. Wellington was buried in the Crypt and 13,000 mourners attended the State Funeral at St Paul's. For years the funeral carriage was on display in the Crypt, but is now on show at the Duke's home at Stratfield Saye.

Many great soldiers are commemorated in the North Aisle. They include the bronze effigy of Major General Charles Gordon (1833-85), who was killed at Khartoum, and his brother Sir Henry (1818-87), Field Marshal Lord Slim (1891-1970) and Field Marshal Earl Roberts (1832-1914).

Apart from the military arts, the creative arts are also remembered. In the North Aisle is a memorial to Lord Leighton (1830-96), the painter and sculptor. His bronze monument is considered one of the outstanding masterpieces of Sir Thomas Brock and one of the details includes a miniature of Leighton's own work, The Sluggard.

The Chapel of St Dunstan *(28)* was the second part of Wren's building to be brought into use in 1699, after the Choir. It is dedicated to Dunstan, a Bishop of London and Archbishop of Canterbury some thousand years ago. Once known as the Morning Chapel, because the early Morning Office was said there prior to the sung service, it features a celebrated wooden entrance screen carved by Jonathan Maine, one of Wren's great craftsmen.

The Chapel of All Souls *(29)*, on the ground floor of the Cathedral's North West Tower, was dedicated in 1925 to the memory of Field Marshal Lord Kitchener (1850-1916) and every other serviceman who died in the 1914-18 World War. The sculpted figures of the military saints, Michael and George, the pieta over the altar and the effigy of Lord Kitchener are by Sir William Reid Dick. The two silver candlesticks on the altar were fashioned from melted down trophies won by members of the London Rifle Brigade.

The Chapel of All Souls, dedicated to the memory of Field Marshal Lord Kitchener (29)

The Crypt

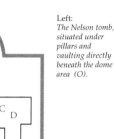

Over the entrance to the Crypt *(30)*, or basement, are carved three death's heads: a reminder of the purpose of the Crypt as a burial place.

The Cathedral's Crypt is the largest in Europe. It is not just massive; its graceful vaulting also makes it one of the most impressive. It was completely restored in the 19th century when some 50 tonnes of grime were cleaned and cleared away.

While burials no longer take place here, some 200 memorials can be seen. They range from the grand and glorious, such as the tombs of Wellington (L) and Nelson (O), to the humble and moving. After he died of his wounds at Trafalgar, the body of Horatio Nelson (1758-1805) was

PLAN OF THE CRYPT & MEMORIAL LOCATION

A. O.B.E. Chapel
B. William Blake
C. Sir Joshua Reynolds
D. Sir Christopher Wren
E. Arthur Sullivan
F. Sir Edwin Lutyens
G. Alfred Gilbert
H. Walter de la Mare
I. Alexander Fleming
   Prof. Gordon
   Hamilton-Fairley
   Sir Henry Wellcome
   John Wycliffe
J. Henry Moore
K. Ivor Novello
L. The Duke of
   Wellington
M. The Treasury
N. Florence Nightingale
O. Admiral Lord Nelson
P. George Washington
Q. Lawrence of Arabia
R. Gulf Memorial
S. Gallipoli Memorial
T. Korean Memorial
U. South Atlantic
V. Shop
W. Cathedral Floor Exit &
   Entrance
X. Crypt Exit & Entrance

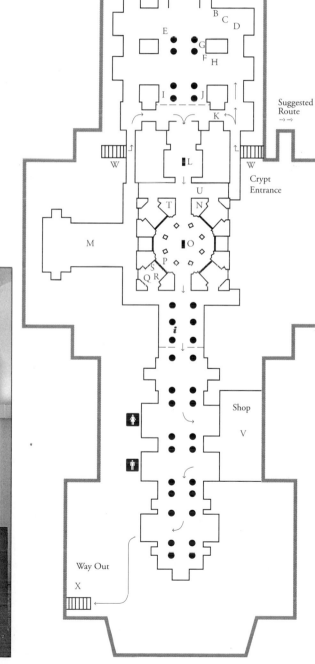

Left:
The Nelson tomb, situated under pillars and vaulting directly beneath the dome area (O).

Suggested
Route
→ →

Crypt
Entrance

Shop

Way Out

preserved in a keg of naval brandy and placed inside four coffins before burial in the Crypt beneath the black marble sarcophagus, originally made three centuries earlier for Cardinal Wolsey. Nelson rests immediately under the

by a terrorist bomb: "It matters not how a man dies but how he lives."

Memorials to those who made distinguished contributions to the arts include Ivor Novello (K), composer; Henry Moore (J), sculptor; Walter de la Mare (H), poet; Max Beerbohm, writer and caricaturist; Sir Edwin Lutyens (F), architect; Sir Joshua Reynolds (C), painter; William Blake (B), artist and poet; Sir Arthur Sullivan (E), the composer of Gilbert and Sullivan fame.

Those who made great contributions to the nation's well-being include Sir Henry Wellcome (I), pharmacist and philanthropist; Sir Alexander Fleming (I), who discovered penicillin; John Wycliffe (I), the 14th century priest and

preacher who translated the Bible into English; and Florence Nightingale (N), the nurse.

There is much in the Crypt that speaks of heroism and bravery, but overwhelmingly the sadness of war is illustrated by the monuments, such as to those who fell in recent conflicts in Korea (T) South Atlantic (U) and the Gulf (R) and remembering those of a former generation who gave their lives in the Gallipoli campaign (S). There is also much which commemorates excellence, inspiration, dedication and craftsmanship.

Top:
The Duke of Wellington's tomb, made of Cornish porphyry (L).

Above:
Memorial to Florence Nightingale, nurse (N).

Bottom Right:
Memorial to the Korean War (T).

Right:
Gulf memorial (R).

centre of the Dome. Wellington's tomb, of Cornish porphyritic granite, is supported by a block of Peterhead granite.

Among the simple and moving monuments is one to Sir Christopher Wren (D). Another is the recent memorial to Professor Gordon Hamilton-Fairley (1930-1975) (I), killed

GALLIPOLI 1915

TO COMMEMORATE
ALL WHO TOOK PART IN
THE GALLIPOLI CAMPAIGN
TO SALUTE THE HEROISM
& FORTITUDE DISPLAYED
AND TO REMEMBER THOSE
WHO DID NOT RETURN

GALLIPOLI PENINSULA

SUBTUS CONDITUR
HUIUS ECCLESIÆ ET VRBIS CONDITOR
CHRISTOPHORUS WREN,
QUI VIXIT ANNOS ULTRA NONAGINTA,
NON SIBI SED BONO PUBLICO.
LECTOR, SI MONUMENTUM REQUIRIS,
CIRCUMSPICE.
Obijt XXV. Feb: An° MDCCXXIII. Æt. XCI.

REMEMBER THE MEN WHO
MADE SHAPELY THE STONES
OF SAINT PAULS CATHEDRAL
1675 – 1708
EDWARD STRONG · THOMAS STRONG
AND ALL WHO LABOURED WITH THEM
This tablet was erected by
The Worshipful Company of Masons

Left:
*On the wall
above Wren's
grave is a plaque
bearing the
simple Latin
epitaph. Below it
is a memorial to
the stonemason
brothers Edward
and Thomas
Strong, involved
in building the
Cathedral (D).*

Far left:
*Gallipoli
memorial (S).*

Below right:
*Plaster bust of
Sir Christopher
Wren.*

Below:
*Block of stone
with Wren's
mark.*

THE OBE CHAPEL

Many services are held in the Crypt's Chapel of the Order of the British Empire, which honours those who have given distinguished service to their country at home or abroad. The Chapel was dedicated at a service attended by the Queen and the Duke of Edinburgh in 1960. There is also a smaller chapel in the Crypt, St Christopher's, a children's chapel. A stained glass panel above the altar depicts St Christopher carrying the Christ child.

THE TREASURY

The Cathedral treasures have been denuded over the centuries: either openly, when seized by the state, or surreptitiously by a major robbery in 1810. On display

Above:
The OBE Chapel, dedicated in 1960 (A).

Right:
Glass panel, depicting Her Majesty Queen Elizabeth, in the OBE Chapel.

Far right
The Crypt contains a children's chapel, St Christopher's. The story of St Paul's Cathedral worked in collage.

Left:
*Some items of
liturgical plate
(M).*

Below left:
*Silver decorations
on Virgers'
Staves (M).*

now are over 200 items of liturgical plate lent by churches in the London diocese, together with examples of the Cathedral's plate and vestments, including the Jubilee Cope of 1977, worn for the service of thanksgiving to mark the 25th anniversary of the coronation of Her Majesty Queen Elizabeth.

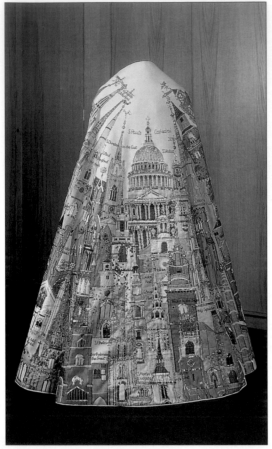

Right:
*The embroidered
Jubilee cope of
1977, designed by
Beryl Dean (M).*

Above right:
*The Treasury
features over 200
items on display
(M).*

Below:
*Locks failed to
secure the
treasures during
a major robbery
in 1810 (M).*

Far right:
*The gift shop is
situated in the
Crypt (V).*

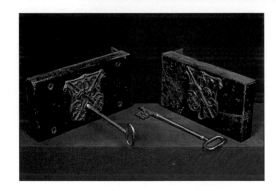

CRYPT FACILITIES

The west end of the Crypt
contains the shop (opened
in April 1995) a cafe,
comfortable toilets and is
soon to have a lecture room
and conference centre. It is
also a venue for occasional
exhibitions.

Facts and Figures

* St Paul is the City of London's patron saint.
* The first St Paul's was built in AD 604.
* The present building was started in 1675 and took 35 years to build.
* It cost £721,552.
* A tax was put on coal coming into London to pay for it.
* St Paul's is a cathedral church, the main church of a diocese.
* It is where the Bishop of London has his throne or 'cathedra'.
* The Cathedral's overall length is 157 metres.
* Its breadth is 76 metres.
* The height of the Dome (to the top of the Cross) is 111 metres.
* The weight of the Dome and superstructure is some 65,000 tonnes.
* There are 530 steps to the Golden Gallery.
* The building stone came from the royal quarries on the Isle of Portland, Dorset. It both carves and weathers well.
* Nearly 150 full and part-time staff are needed to run St Paul's.
* Between one to two million visitors a year have been welcomed.

* On a summer's day it has been calculated that 40,000 visitors give off a million and a half kilocalories of heat inside the Cathedral .
* Great Paul, Britain's heaviest swinging bell (17 tonnes), rings daily for five minutes at 1 o'clock.
* The Cathedral clock Big Tom is of similar size to Westminster's Big Ben.
* The clock's three dials have minute hands nearly three metres long.
* It costs around £5 million a year (£10 a minute) to run and maintain St Paul's.

* The first admission fee was introduced in 1709 – before the Cathedral was complete.
* There are now nearly 300 monuments within the Cathedral including one to its architect, Sir Christopher Wren. He wanted none.
* The organ, has five keyboards, 138 stops and 7,189 pipes.
* The Library has some 27,000 books, sermons and pamphlets.
* The Crypt, or basement area, is the largest in Europe.

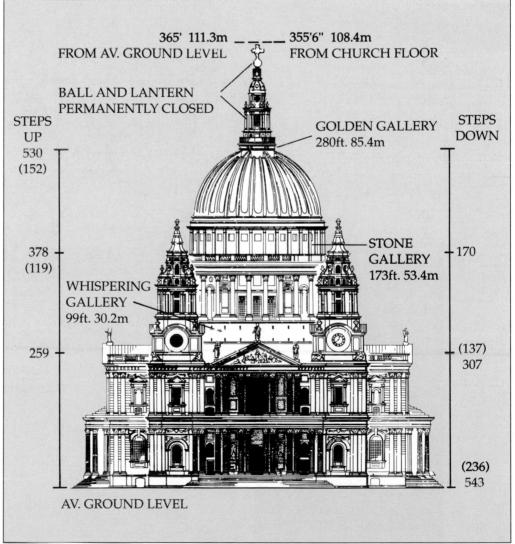

31

Chapel of St Dunstan

*The Light of
the World*

The Dome and
Whispering Gallery

Organ

Tijou Gates

The High
Altar

Exterior and Churchyard

Below:
The Cathedral's West Front.

Below right:
West Front statue of St Paul above a bas-relief showing his conversion.

S t Paul's was largely created and carved from stone from the royal quarries at Portland in Dorset. Ships brought it around the south coast and up the River Thames to Paul's Wharf at the foot of Peter's Hill.

WEST FRONT

Two storeys of dignified classical columns, flanked by twin towers, provide a stone frame for the central dramatic frontispiece of St Paul's: a pediment featuring a bas-relief sculpture of the Conversion of St Paul. Above the pediment, carved by Francis Bird, stands a figure of St Paul himself. In his hand he carries a sword, which is his emblem. To either side are figures of St Peter and St James – two of the ring of apostles at roof level around the Cathedral. These too are the

work of Francis Bird (1667-1731).

Panels above the Great West Door entrance show scenes from the life and works of St Paul.

The twin towers house the bells and the clock. Big Tom is the popular name of the clock with three dials (each more than 5 metres in diameter) in the south-

the clock is now automatically wound and the chiming parts driven by electric motors. The 'ding-dong' quarter chimes are struck on two 18th century bells. The hours are struck on a large bell, called Great Tom, dating from 1716. As well as striking the hours, it tolls the deaths of royalty, the Archbishop of Canterbury, the Bishop of London, the Dean of St Paul's and the Lord Mayor of London.

Great Paul is the name of the Cathedral's biggest bell. At 17 tonnes, it is Britain's heaviest swinging bell. It is nearly three metres in diameter at the base and is tolled daily at 1 o'clock. In the north-west tower is the ring of 12 bells of St Paul's whose peal is considered one of the finest in the country. They are rung on Sundays and for festivals by St Paul's Cathedral Guild of Ringers, a group of 30 volunteers.

In the forecourt of the Cathedral is a statue of Queen Anne, who was the reigning monarch when the building was completed.

Left:
View of London from the Dome's Stone Gallery.

Below:
St Paul's length is 157 metres.

Below left:
Big Tom, the Cathedral clock.

west tower. It is of similar design and size to the Westminster clock, Big Ben. The first clock, dating from 1708, had to be replaced in 1719. The present one was made and installed by John Smith and Sons of Derby and dates from 1893. In 1969, a modernised mechanism was installed so that

CHURCHYARD

Over the south portico of the Cathedral the pediment, carved by Caius Gabriel Cibber, displays a phoenix (symbol of resurrection) with the word RESURGAM. The pediment of the north portico features the Royal arms.

At the north-east corner of the Cathedral churchyard is Paul's Cross Memorial. Designed by Sir Reginald Blomfield, it was erected in 1910 and consists of a Tuscan column on which stands a sculpture of St Paul. It represents the site where

open air sermons were preached. (The original Paul's Cross is marked by an inscription on the ground nearby.)

Far right:
St Paul's Cross, where open air sermons were once preached.

Right:
The South Portico featuring the phoenix, symbol of resurrection.

Below:
View from the south side of the Thames of St Paul's illuminated against the City skyline.

Behind The Scenes

Virgers of St Paul's.

St Paul's is not only a place of regular worship and pilgrimage, but also a valuable part of the nation's heritage. Keeping it running and maintained is the job of a dedicated team of people with a variety of skills and professional experience. Some work full-time, others part-time. Many contribute their time and expertise voluntarily.

THE CLERGY

The Governing Body of the Cathedral is the Dean and Chapter which comprises the Dean the Archdeacon of London and the three Residentiary Canons who are known severally as Precentor, Treasurer and Chancellor, they are assisted by the College of Minor Canons. There is also a Greater Chapter composed of the Dean and Chapter and the 30 Prebendaries who work in parishes throughout the Diocese and are appointed by the Bishop of London. Other clergy help voluntarily as chaplains, and sisters from religious communities assist at Holy Communion and can be found in the Cathedral most days.

THE LAY STAFF

More than 120 lay people are employed at St Paul's on a full or part time basis. The team is lead by the Registrar who heads the administrative side of the Cathedral's affairs and implements policies decided by the Chapter. He works closely with the heads of departments, the Surveyor to the Fabric, the Clerk of the Works, the Administrative Manager, the Financial Controller, the Secretary of the Friends, the Retail Manager, the Dean's Virger, the Visits Officer and the Catering Manager; and each of these in turn looks after a large body of skilled workstaff, stewards, virgers, shop assistants, catering assistants, secretaries and many volunteers who man our welcome desk and conduct tours of the cathedral. We have a team of bellringers who give their services voluntarily Sunday by Sunday.

Left: The Dean and Chapter of St Paul's.

MUSIC

Music plays a large part in the life of the Cathedral. In addition to the Organist and Director of Music, the Sub-Organist and Assistant Organist, there are 18 men singers called Vicars Choral, and 38 boy choristers who are educated in the Cathedral Choir School, one of the few remaining in England. This has its own Headmaster and teaching staff.

THE LIBRARY

Directly over the Chapel of St Michael and St George is the Cathedral Library. It has remained virtually unchanged since its completion in 1709. The woodblock floor by Charles Hopson, the carved brackets under the gallery by Jonathan Maine, the stone pilasters carved by William Kempster on the gallery and the oak presses in which the

Below:
Choristers of the St Paul's Cathedral Choir School & above as young musicians.

Main picture:
Cathedral library.

Inset:
Model of Wellington's funeral carriage in the Library.

and commentaries, service and liturgical books. Henry Compton, London's Bishop during the building of St Paul's, left almost 2,000 books to the Library in his will. The oldest book in the Library is a service book which was used in Old St Paul's and was written over 800 years ago. The rarest is a first edition of William Tyndale's New Testament, 1525, one of only two copies in the world. While the Cathedral manuscripts were moved to the Guildhall Library in 1980 where they are now preserved at the correct temperature and humidity, the job of cleaning, checking, maintaining and re-cataloguing the library stock remains an important one.

books are shelved are all in their original state.

While the Library is not open to view by the general public, staff undertake research on behalf of the Dean and Chapter.

The Library is now rich in rare books, particularly Bibles, New Testaments, concordances

Above:
The Cathedral's oldest book, written over 800 years ago.

Left:
Henry Compton, Bishop of London when Wren's cathedral was being built.

CRAFTSMEN

The Works Department is responsible for the Cathedral's maintenance, for the Chapter House, the Choir School and the residential houses in nearby Amen Court. It includes stonemasons, carvers, carpenter, plumber, painters, electricians, scaffolders and a general duty gang.

FRIENDS OF ST PAUL'S

The Friends of St Paul's, who number over 4,000 from Britain

Top:
Cathedral stonemasons.

Above right:
Oiling the clock mechanism to keep the City on time.

Right:
A woodcarver working to preserve the Cathedral's heritage.

Below:
A steward assisting two of our visitors on the stone gallery.

and around the world, give valuable financial and practical support to the Cathedral. They welcome visitors, act as guides and supply help and information on a daily basis. Gifts made possible by members' annual subscriptions have enriched and enhanced the Cathedral over the years.

They have their origin in the Watch, a devoted band of volunteers through whose nightly vigilance during wartime St Paul's largely owes its survival.

If you are interested in becoming a Friend, write to the Secretary, Friends of St Paul's, Chapter House, St Paul's Churchyard, London EC4M 8AD.

Above:
The Geometrical Staircase, designed by Wren and built and carved by William Kempster with ironwork by Jean Tijou.

Left:
Statue to the members of the National Fire Service who fought to save the City and many other major centres of population from destruction during the Second World War.

Below left:
Framed by the smoke and fire of the Blitz, the Dome of St Paul's became a symbol of the nation's indomitable spirit.

The History of St Paul's

When digging the foundations for the present Cathedral building, architect Sir Christopher Wren made an interesting discovery. He wrote: "Here we discovered Quantities of Urns, broken Vessels and Pottery-ware of diverse Sorts and Shapes".

He also found "Graves of several Ages and Fashions in strata, or Layers of Earth one above the other, particularly at the North side of Paul's (which) manifestly shew'd a great Antiquity from the British and Roman Times."

THE FIRST ST PAUL'S

A wooden cathedral, dedicated to St Paul, was built on the site in AD 604 for Mellitus, Bishop of the East Saxons. Mellitus was one of the second wave of missionaries sent to England by Pope Gregory the Great. Ethelbert, King of Kent, founded the Cathedral and endowed it with the Manor of Tillingham in Essex, a property which remains in the possession

Right:
Lightning twice destroyed the spire of Old St Paul's. A 1650 view.

Below:
The late Saxon church of St Paul.

of the Dean and Chapter to this day.

The Saxon church was destroyed by fire and rebuilt a number of times. After the last disaster in 1087, the Normans undertook to construct a massive church whose size and style reflected the importance of London in their newly conquered kingdom.

OLD ST PAUL'S

The Cathedral, in grand and Gothic style, was at the heart of everyday life in the City of London. Paul's Cross in the Cathedral grounds became an open-air pulpit for preachers. Political debates, general assemblies and even trials were held there. Old St Paul's was the largest church in England and the third largest in Europe. It boasted the tallest spire and steeple ever built in England – and these features were to become instrumental in its decline and decay after lightning did strike in the same place twice.

Brave attempts were made to combat the effects of natural disasters and neglect, but the Great Fire of 1666 put the Cathedral completely beyond restoration.

Old St Paul's.

*The Great Fire of
London, 1666, by
Phillippe de
Louthebourg
(1740-1812)*

RESURRECTION UNDER WREN

The man chosen in 1669 to design and construct a new St Paul's was Christopher Wren. He was not only an architect, but also a Latinist, scientist, anatomist, astronomer, mathematician and engineer. Son of a dean and nephew of a bishop, he was also a deeply religious and humane man.

Pembroke College Chapel, Cambridge, was the first building Wren designed. The date was 1661. This was followed by a celebrated masterpiece – the Sheldonian Theatre in Oxford, built between 1664-9.

While the Great Plague raged in London in 1665, Wren travelled to France to study buildings, especially the Louvre in Paris. The Great Fire of London the following year brought Wren to the architectural fore back home.

He was appointed by King Charles II as one of the three commissioners to survey the extent of the damage and to advise how the City should be rebuilt. A tax was put on coal coming into the Port of London to pay for rebuilding 52 churches in the City. This scheme later financed the building of St Paul's.

Wren's first design was rejected outright: while he had attempted to give London a new cathedral that would be inexpensive to build yet handsome in appearance, it was thought to be untraditional. His second design was more ambitious and a model was made (now on display in the Trophy Room) for £600. While the King approved, the Church authorities disagreed and dithered. Finally, the King issued

a warrant of approval to allow the project to proceed. This also gave Wren the freedom to vary the design if needed.

Wren's inventive mind turned to speeding up the work of demolishing the old Cathedral. He suggested small charges of gunpowder to help topple the massive tower pillars which stood over 65 metres high. When the explosions produced complaints from the public, battering rams were used to knock the pillars down. With the site at last cleared, work on the new Cathedral could begin.

BUILDING ST PAUL'S

Wren himself insisted on supervising the preliminary measurements. While he was fixing on the ground the position of the Cathedral's crowning masterpiece, the Dome, he called for a stone to mark the place. A workman brought him a flat stone from a nearby heap of rubble. Wren turned it over and saw that it was a gravestone fragment from the ruins of Old St Paul's. Carved on the stone, in large capitals, was the single Latin word RESURGAM – 'I shall rise again'.

Throughout the 35 years of building work, Wren supervised, engaged the finest craftsmen, scrutinised and signed the accounts and visited the site each Saturday. Presumably to prevent interference, he insisted that the work be carried out under conditions of some secrecy, with whole sections under wraps.

Early in 1697 Parliament, prodded by those who believed the project was proceeding too slowly, suspended half of Wren's annual salary until the Cathedral was completed. This was in 1710.

Wren died on 25 February 1723, his 91st year, having (as he wrote) "worn out, by God's Mercy, a long life in the Royal Service, and have made some Figure in the World". He was buried in the Crypt of St Paul's, with a simple but sublime epitaph.

HR: WREN.
EYOR GENERAL - of
al Buildings .
4. of Feb. 1723, aged 91.

G. Kneller p.1711.

Left:
Portrait of Sir Christopher Wren, St Paul's architect. Painted by Sir Godfrey Kneller, 1711.

Top left:
View of St Paul's a century and a half ago, seen from across the River Thames at Bankside. Painted by William Richardson (1842-1877).

Below left:
Sir Christopher Wren was hauled up to the top of the Dome in a basket to inspect progress.

You're Welcome

Within the awesome grandeur of Wren's architectural masterpiece, the simple act of Christian worship is carried on every day, just as it has been on this site for over a thousand years.

Please come and join us.

Our regular services are held on weekdays at 07.30 (Said Matins), 08.00 (Holy Communion), 12.30 (Holy Communion), 17.00 (Choral Evensong).

On Sundays at 08.00 (Holy Communion), 08.45 (Said Matins), 11.00 (Sung Eucharist) and 15.15 (Choral Evensong).

The Choir sings on Sundays at 11.00 and 15.15 and on weekdays at 17.00. These service times are published as a guide only.

Please telephone our information line to avoid disappointment 0171 246 8348.

As well as daily worship, baptisms, weddings, and special services – some of national importance – are regularly held at St Paul's.

Top right:
The Dean with The Ambassador of the United States of America and Mrs Crowe. Thanksgiving Day Service Reception November 1996.

Above:
Every year, St Paul's is the focus for an important event in the City of London, the Lord Mayor's Show.

Right:
Services of worship have been held at the St Paul's site since AD 604.